Copyright © 2019 by L. Miller
All rights reserved. No part of this publication may be reproduced or used in any manner without written permission of the copyright owner except for the use of quotations in a book review.

DEDICATION

I dedicate this book to my daughter, Leonna, whom my words are always written for. You are the external duplicate of my heart. I will always keep you spiritually fortified, and I promise to always speak knowledge and all the love a mother can give, into your life.

HOW WE PRAY
L. MILLER

Mother

Say your prayers before you eat, Beloved.

Mother

Say your prayers before you sleep, Beloved.

Daughter

Umm....

Daughter

Mama, how do we pray?

Mother

What do you mean, Beloved?

Daughter

You tell me all the time to pray to the Most High God, but I don't know what to pray about.

Mother

Well, when you pray, you start off by giving thanks to the Most High. The one who created you.

Daughter

How do I do that?

Mother

You tell God what you are thankful for in your life. It can be good, or it can be bad.

Daughter
Bad?! Why would I thank God for the bad stuff, Mama?

Mother
You are very smart to ask that question. Think of the bad stuff as lessons that the Most High teaches you. You use those lessons to become smarter and stronger. It will teach you to find a good thing in any bad thing. But don't worry, because you will understand better as you get older.

Daughter
OK, Mama. I will pray and thank God now.

Daughter

Thank you God, for my....

Mother

Beloved, are you still praying?

Daughter

Yes, Mama. I have not finished thanking God for each one of my toys and games.

Mother

Beloved, you do not have to thank God for each item you have. You can give thanks to God for your possessions, but it is also important to give thanks for your life, the people in your life, and the things that you learn every day to help you as you grow older and smarter. You can speak to God about any subject. Your prayers will always be heard... I also have a secret to share with you...

Daughter
What secret, Mama?

Mother
So your prayers won't be so long at night, you can pray throughout the whole day, anytime you want to speak to God. Just close your eyes to keep you from distraction, then bow your head or kneel on your knees, to show you will submit in the presence of our God, who is always listening.

Mother

Goodnight, Beloved. I love you!

Daughter

Goodnight, Mama. I love you too!

Daughter

Hello, God. It's me again. Thank you for my Mama. She is the best.

AMEN

BONUS PAGE:
ACTIVITY TIME

Speak to your child about prayer and how you pray. It will lead them to take up their own prayers and allow them spiritual growth.

ACKNOWLEDGEMENTS

To my father, Wayne, who watched over my precious Leonna in my stead. While I was deployed overseas to Afghanistan, you made it so much easier for me to get through the days, knowing that she was well cared for. I had enough peace of mind while there, to write this book. Thank you.

To my mother, Corlette, I give my thanks for your continued support, and always having my back.

To Leonna's grandparents: Tonya and Robert. I couldn't have asked for better co-grandparents. You two have always been the best to Leonna and I. From the moment she was born, you have shown her infinite love. Thank you so much.

Last but certainly not least, I want to give a special, humble thank you to the creator of my soul. You breathed life into my body, and made me strong enough to get through the toughest situations. My path is mine, but my soul and aura are of your making. I thank you for my endurance and pure heart, my God.

Made in the USA
Las Vegas, NV
08 November 2021